WITHDRAWN

KARATE
in Action

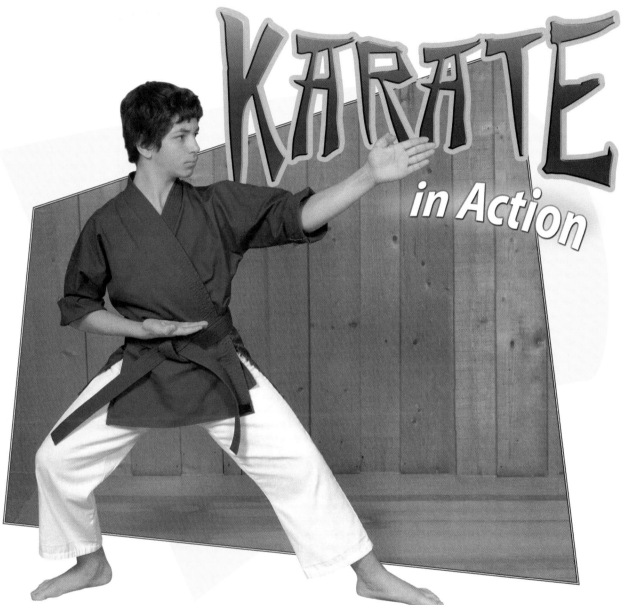

Kelley MacAulay & Bobbie Kalman
🌳 Crabtree Publishing Company
www.crabtreebooks.com

Created by Bobbie Kalman

Dedicated by Kelley MacAulay
For Fred Humphrey and the Karma Kagyu Meditation Centre of Niagara,
For your guidance, encouragement, and friendship

Editor-in-Chief
Bobbie Kalman

Writing team
Kelley MacAulay
Bobbie Kalman

Substantive editor
Kathryn Smithyman

Editors
Molly Aloian
Robin Johnson
Reagan Miller

Design
Vanessa Parson-Robbs
Samantha Crabtree (cover)

Production coordinator
Heather Fitzpatrick

Photo research
Crystal Foxton

Consultant
Deborah Toth, Fourth Degree Black Belt
Goju Ryu Karate Do

Special thanks to
Christian DiCienzo, Lucia Leone, Philippe Marquis, Daniel Puhl,
Dandi Yang, John Siemens, Jerry Leone, Deborah Toth, and
The Martial Arts Center

Illustrations
Katherine Kantor: pages 6, 10, 11, 28
Bonna Rouse: pages 7, 8, 9

Photographs
All photographs by Marc Crabtree except:
David Bolsover Photography Sheffield UK: pages 30, 31

Crabtree Publishing Company

www.crabtreebooks.com   1-800-387-7650

Cataloging-in-Publication Data
MacAulay, Kelley.
  Karate in action / Kelley MacAulay & Bobbie Kalman; photographs by
Marc Crabtree.
    p. cm. -- (Sports in action series)
  Includes index.
  ISBN-13: 978-0-7787-0341-9 (rlb)
  ISBN-10: 0-7787-0341-X (rlb)
  ISBN-13: 978-0-7787-0361-7 (pbk)
  ISBN-10: 0-7787-0361-4 (pbk)
  1. Karate--Juvenile literature. I. Kalman, Bobbie. II. Title. III. Sports in action.
  GV1114.3.M323 2006
  796.815'3--dc22
                                                        2005020741
                                                             LC

**Published in
the United States**
PMB16A
350 Fifth Ave.
Suite 3308
New York, NY
10118

**Published
in Canada**
616 Welland Ave.,
St. Catharines, Ontario,
Canada
L2M 5V6

**Published in the
United Kingdom**
73 Lime Walk
Headington
Oxford
OX3 7AD
United Kingdom

**Published
in Australia**
386 Mt. Alexander Rd.,
Ascot Vale (Melbourne)
VIC 3032

Contents

What is karate? 空手

Karate is a Japanese **martial art**, or method of fighting created for use as self-defense. In Japanese, the word "karate" means "empty hands," or fighting without the use of weapons. Students of karate learn how to perform **techniques**, or skilled motions. Students use these techniques to gain control over **opponents**. Karate students must learn more than just physical skills, however! They are also taught valuable lessons about **self-discipline**. These lessons show karate students how to use their bodies and minds together to achieve their personal best.

A long history

Karate began hundreds of years ago on the small Japanese island called Okinawa. At that time, the government in Okinawa banned its people from using weapons of any kind. To protect their homes and families, some Okinawans began training secretly in "empty-handed" fighting. Over time, more and more people learned this fighting method, which became known as karate. Today, karate is one of the most popular martial arts in the world!

Although karate is a method of fighting, students use their skills only for self-defense.

A code of behavior

Karate students must follow a code of proper behavior when they are in their *dojos*, or training halls. One of the most important elements of this behavior is respect. Students must be respectful of their dojos, their *senseis*, or instructors, and of other students. One way students show respect is by bowing to greet their senseis. Students also show respect by keeping their dojos tidy and by helping other students.

Reaching your goals

Karate students spend years training to become skilled at karate. Although some students take part in competitions as they improve their skills, many students train only to reach their own personal goals. Winning competitions is exciting, but each student's main goal should be to perform always at his or her personal best.

Your sensei will teach you how to set goals for yourself and will guide you as you work to achieve your goals.

The essentials 空手

Before you can become a student of karate, you must choose a dojo. Most dojos emphasize either **traditional karate** or **sport karate**. Dojos that emphasize traditional karate focus on teaching traditional self-defense, as well as self-discipline and proper behavior.

Dojos that emphasize sport karate focus on preparing students to compete in karate competitions. Are you interested in taking part in karate competitions? If not, you may want to choose a karate dojo that teaches traditional karate.

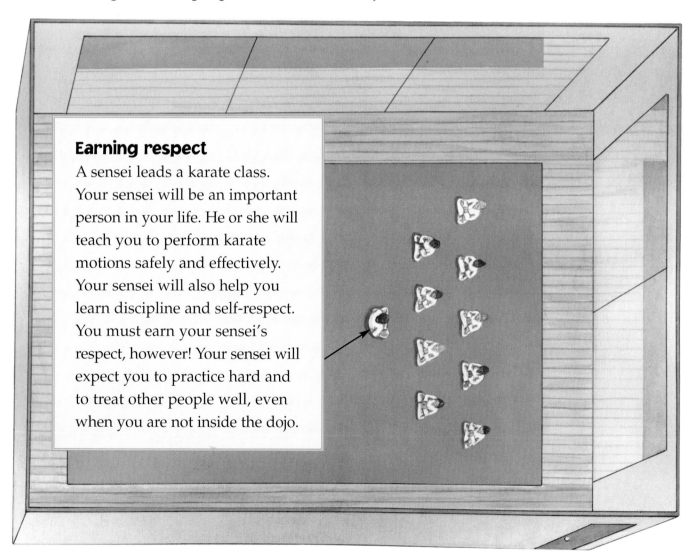

Earning respect
A sensei leads a karate class. Your sensei will be an important person in your life. He or she will teach you to perform karate motions safely and effectively. Your sensei will also help you learn discipline and self-respect. You must earn your sensei's respect, however! Your sensei will expect you to practice hard and to treat other people well, even when you are not inside the dojo.

Your uniform

A karate student trains and competes in a uniform called a *gi*. A gi consists of a jacket and loose-fitting pants. Traditionally, gis were white, but today students can wear colorful gis. Some students also wear white t-shirts under their jackets. You must take good care of your gi. Wearing a dirty or a torn gi shows a lack of respect for your dojo and for your sensei.

Shoes are not permitted in the training area of a dojo. Students train in bare feet.

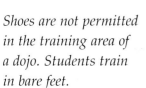

Belts of many colors

A karate uniform is tied at the waist by an *obi*, or belt. The belt for each level of karate is a different color. Beginner students wear white belts. Each time a student advances to a new level of training, he or she receives a belt of a different color. Students must work hard and pass tests to earn each new belt color.

Kyus

The first group of belt colors are called *kyus*. The belt colors shown right are the traditional kyu colors. Many dojos now use other belt colors between these colors. For example, a student who is not ready to receive his or her green belt may instead be given a red belt. It takes most students three to five years to earn all their kyus.

Black belts

Once students have earned all their kyus, they are ready to earn their first black belts. There are ten black-belt levels, which are called *dans*. Earning each dan requires greater skills and years of practice.

white belt

yellow belt

orange belt

green belt

blue belt

brown belt

black belt

Warming up 空手

Your sensei will begin each class with a series of warm-ups and strengthening exercises. Karate motions can be challenging to perform, and warming up your body helps prevent injuries. Begin by walking briskly for a few minutes to get your heart pumping. Next, do the stretches shown on this page. Remember not to stretch too far! These exercises will become easier as you practice. Once you have stretched, do the strengthening exercises on the next page. They will help you build strong muscles. Having strong muscles helps you perform karate motions safely and effectively.

Quadriceps stretch
Stand on your left foot. Lift up your right foot behind you until you can grab it with your right hand. Keep your knees together. You will feel a stretch in the front of your right leg. Hold the stretch as you count to ten and then switch legs.

"V" stretch
Sit with your legs in a "V" position. **Flex** your feet so your toes are pointing upward. Keeping your back straight, lean forward until you feel a stretch in the back of your legs and buttocks. Hold the stretch as you count to ten.

Front splits
Ease into the front splits by extending your legs as far to the sides as possible. Make sure the inside edges of your feet are on the floor. Place your hands on the floor in front of you and lean slightly forward. Hold this position as you count to 20.

Crunches

To perform a crunch, lie on your back and put your hands behind your head. Bend your knees and place your feet flat on the floor. Press your lower back against the floor as you lift your shoulders slightly off the floor. Lower yourself back down. Repeat ten times.

Pushups

Lie on your stomach. Place your hands flat on the floor beneath your shoulders. Use your arms to push yourself up. Be sure to keep your back flat. Lower yourself until your nose is about four inches (10 cm) from the floor. Repeat ten times. If you find the movement too difficult with your legs extended, keep your knees on the floor as you push up.

Calming meditation

Some senseis also have their students perform **meditations** at the beginning of each class. A meditation is an exercise that focuses your mind and calms you. To meditate, sit quietly on the floor with your legs crossed. Make sure your back is straight. Close your eyes and breathe deeply, focusing on each breath you take. After meditating, most students are able to concentrate better on their karate techniques.

The first step 空手

Before students can perform karate motions, they must first be able to hold their hands and feet in the correct positions. Different motions require different hand or foot positions. Each position allows a different part of your body to strike your opponent with the greatest force. For example, when you strike an opponent with your fist, a certain part of your fist will strike the opponent's body with the greatest force. By holding your hands and feet in the correct positions, you will ensure that your motions are effective, and that they are also safe for you to perform. You will use the hand and foot positions shown on these pages again and again.

1. The most frequently used hand position is the fist. To make a fist, curl your fingers tightly into your palm.

2. Next, press your thumb against the outside of your first two fingers. In this position, the knuckles on your fist provide the greatest striking force.

*To make **knife-hand** position, straighten your fingers and press them together. Curl the tips of your fingers slightly inward. Curling your fingers helps prevent injuries. Bend your thumb and press it against the edge of your hand. When your hand is in knife-hand position, the outside edge of your hand provides the greatest striking force.*

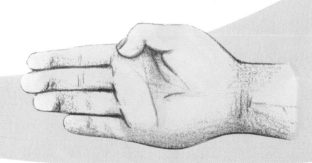

Foot positions

Foot positions refer to the area of the foot that is used to perform a motion. To control which part of your foot makes contact with your opponent, you must bend your foot in a specific direction. Be sure to hold the position when your foot makes contact with your opponent!

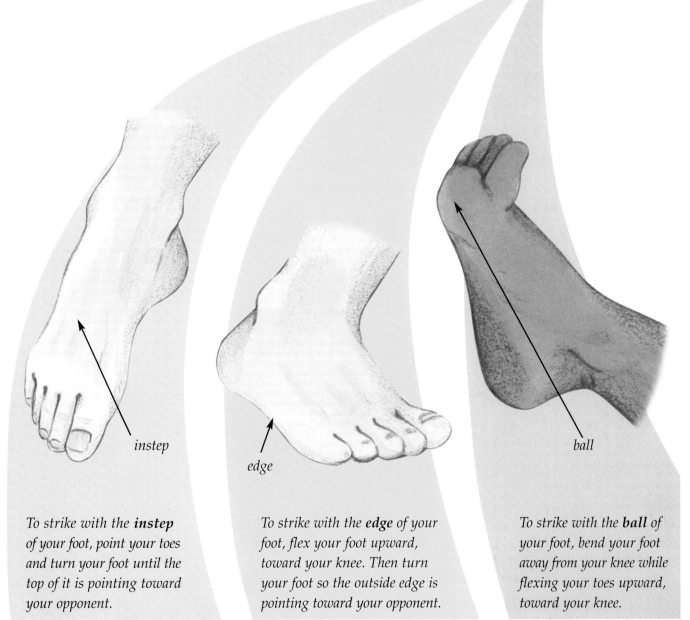

instep

edge

ball

To strike with the **instep** of your foot, point your toes and turn your foot until the top of it is pointing toward your opponent.

To strike with the **edge** of your foot, flex your foot upward, toward your knee. Then turn your foot so the outside edge is pointing toward your opponent.

To strike with the **ball** of your foot, bend your foot away from your knee while flexing your toes upward, toward your knee.

Take your positions 空手

Some of the first positions karate students learn are called **stances**. A stance is made up of the positions of your feet, legs, and upper body as you stand. Stances are the basic building blocks of all karate motions. Having a solid stance allows you to perform karate motions with force. By practicing your stances often, you will increase your balance, coordination, and **stability**. You will also learn to move from one stance to another. By changing stances, you will be able to perform **combinations** (see page 20). These pages show some basic karate stances that all students learn.

Forward stance

Stand in ready stance (see page 13) and take a large step forward with your left foot. Bend your left knee until you can see only the tip of your big toe. Keep your back leg straight. Point your left foot straight ahead. Turn your right foot out slightly. Close your hands into fists. Extend your left arm out in front of you. Pull your right arm to belt level, with your palm pointing upward. In some dojos, students are taught to hold their right arms higher, at armpit level.

Horse stance

Stand with your legs spread twice as wide as the width of your shoulders. Turn your feet out slightly and bend your knees. Keep your back straight. Hold your arms in front of your body, with your elbows slightly bent. Close your hands into fists and hold them between your thighs.

Ready stance

From ready stance, you can defend your body from any direction. Stand with your legs about shoulder-width apart. Bend your knees slightly. Close your hands tightly into fists and hold them in front of you at thigh level.

Back stance

Stand in ready stance and take a large step back with your right foot. Turn your right foot until your toes are pointing to the side. Keep your left foot pointing forward. Bend your knees. Point your upper body in the direction of your right foot. Keep your head facing in the direction of your left foot. Hold your hands in knife-hand position. Place your right hand in front of your stomach with your palm pointing upward. Extend your left arm out to the side in the same direction as that of your left foot.

Punches and strikes 空手

Hand techniques are often a karate student's quickest form of attack. Hand techniques consist of **punches** and **strikes**. A punch is any technique used by the attacker to force his or her hand directly at an opponent. A strike is any hand technique used by the attacker to hit his or her opponent from the side, from above, or from below.

Adding force

Every punch or strike is made more effective by using **reaction**. As your attacking arm is thrust out, quickly pull your opposite arm back toward your body. Rotate your hips along with your arms to shift your weight into the motion. For example, as you punch, roll one hip forward and the other hip backward. Remember to hold your wrist stiff as your hand connects with your opponent. Pull your attacking arm back immediately after striking your opponent, to make sure he or she does not have a chance to grab your arm.

*Beginners should throw slow, careful punches and strikes as they learn to control the direction of their movements. Hand techniques should be powerful and strong, but they will be of no use if a student cannot control where the techniques land. This student is performing a **reverse punch**.*

1. To perform a **knife-hand strike**, begin in back stance. With your hands in knife-hand position, raise your right arm until your hand is close to the side of your head. Keep your palm turned away from your body.

2. In one swift movement, swing your right arm forward until it is extended in front of you, with your palm pointing upward. Keep your arm slightly bent as you perform the motion. The inside edge of your hand provides the greatest striking force.

Raise your voice!

As a karate student performs a powerful motion such as a punch, a strike, or a kick, he or she sometimes lets out a *kiai*. A kiai is a sharply exhaled breath accompanied by a loud yell. To perform a kiai, tighten your stomach muscles and force out the breath from your lungs. By performing a kiai, you add force to your motion. A kiai can also startle or frighten your opponent and throw him or her off guard, giving you an advantage.

Karate kicks 空手

The best karate students are those who can defend themselves equally well with their hands and their feet. Although punches and strikes are usually a student's quickest forms of defense, kicks are more powerful. The muscles in your legs are much stronger than the muscles in your arms. Your legs are also longer than your arms, so kicks allow you to keep some distance between yourself and your opponent.

Strength and stamina

Performing kicks requires a lot of **stamina**. Stamina is the energy it takes to perform a move over and over again without becoming tired. Practicing your kicks is the best way to develop the skill and energy needed to perform kicks effectively. As you practice, you will find that you perform kicks better with one leg than with the other. It is important that you continue to practice kicks with both legs, however. Performing kicks equally well with both legs allows you to defend both sides of your body. Your opponent will also never be sure from which side your kick will come!

*Kicks are the most difficult karate motions to master. As you perform a kick, you must be aware of your entire body, as it is easy to lose your balance. This student is performing a **side kick**.*

1. To perform a **front kick**, begin in forward stance. Bring your back leg forward until your knee is level with your hips, bending your knee as you lift. Bend your foot away from the knee, pulling your toes backward toward the knee.

1. To perform a **roundhouse kick**, begin in forward stance. Raise your back leg until your knee is at hip level. Lean your upper body away from your opponent as you raise your leg. Your raised foot and knee should be level with your hip. As you perform the kick, turn the foot on which you are standing until it is pointing away from your opponent.

2. Quickly snap your raised leg forward, holding your leg as high as possible. The ball of your foot provides the greatest striking force.

2. Swing your raised foot upward and outward from the knee as fast as possible.

Basic blocks 空手

Karate is an art of self-defense, so **blocks** are important techniques. A block is a defensive motion that stops an attacker's move from striking your body. The goal of a block is not to stop your opponent's motion altogether. Instead, you want to redirect the opponent's energy by **deflecting** the attack. Most students use their arms to block, but some blocks are performed using the legs. The block you choose will depend on which part of your body is being attacked. With practice, you will learn to watch your opponent so carefully that you will be able to guess which move he or she will make next!

Count on counterattacks

It is important to follow your block with a quick **counterattack**. The power of your block can break your opponent's concentration, or possibly throw him or her off balance. While your opponent is off balance, you can throw a swift kick, punch, or strike, and take control of the **match**.

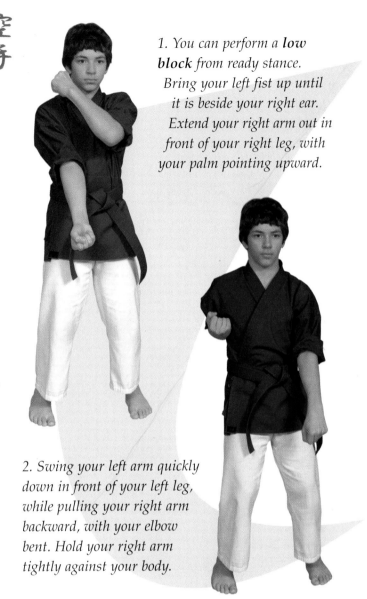

*1. You can perform a **low block** from ready stance. Bring your left fist up until it is beside your right ear. Extend your right arm out in front of your right leg, with your palm pointing upward.*

2. Swing your left arm quickly down in front of your left leg, while pulling your right arm backward, with your elbow bent. Hold your right arm tightly against your body.

Protect both sides

As with other karate motions, it is important to perform blocks well using both your right arm and your left arm. If you can successfully block motions with both arms, you will be able to defend both sides of your body.

1. You can perform a **middle block** from ready stance. Bring your right arm across your body, until your right fist is in front of your left shoulder. Then bring your left arm across your body until your left fist is beneath the upper part of your right arm.

1. You can perform an **upper block** from forward stance. Bring your left arm across your body until your left fist is in front of your right shoulder. Then bring your right fist across your body until your right fist is beneath the upper part of your left arm.

2. Quickly pull your left arm out in front of your body, with your fist at shoulder level. As you move your left arm, pull your right arm backward as far as possible.

2. Quickly pull your left elbow backward as you thrust your right fist into the air. Your hand should be just above your head. Twist the wrist of your raised arm so that your palm is pointing toward your opponent.

Bringing it all together 空手

Combinations are two or more motions performed one right after the other. Knowing how to link motions together is important once you begin to fight against an opponent. If your first motion fails, you have another motion ready to go! When you begin to combine techniques, it is important that you maintain focus on each individual motion. If you are thinking about the second motion you are going to perform as you perform the first motion, the first motion will not be effective. There are many combinations from which to choose. Try practicing different combinations until you discover which ones best suit your abilities.

1. A good combination for beginners is a block followed by a punch. Begin in forward stance and perform a middle block.

*2. Follow your block with a swift **lunge punch**. Step forward with your right leg and thrust your right fist straight out in front of you. As you move your right arm forward, pull your left arm back tightly toward your left armpit.*

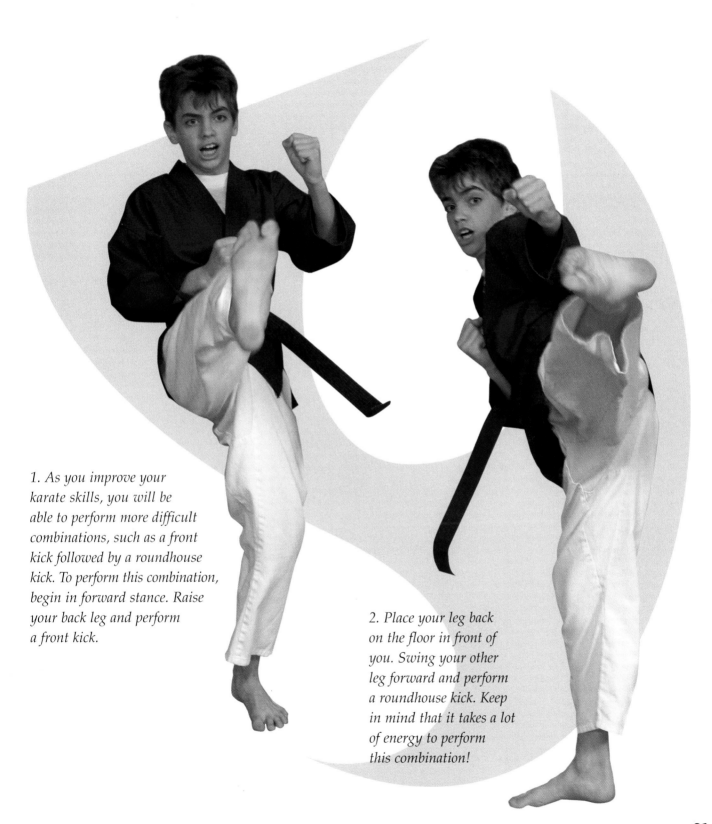

1. As you improve your karate skills, you will be able to perform more difficult combinations, such as a front kick followed by a roundhouse kick. To perform this combination, begin in forward stance. Raise your back leg and perform a front kick.

2. Place your leg back on the floor in front of you. Swing your other leg forward and perform a roundhouse kick. Keep in mind that it takes a lot of energy to perform this combination!

Karate katas 空手

Karate *katas* or **forms** are known as "the heart of karate." Katas are a series of motions, such as punches, strikes, and kicks, arranged in a specific pattern. The pattern allows the motions to flow into one another. A student must learn a new kata to advance to each new belt level. As the belt levels become more advanced, additional techniques are added to the katas. Katas are the artistic moves of karate. You will not advance to the next belt level if you simply memorize the motions in a kata. You must also perform the kata gracefully and put plenty of effort into practicing.

A challenging art

Performing different katas requires a student to have different skills. To perform some katas, a student will need to have strong, lean muscles. Other katas require good coordination. Katas are performed individually, but it is helpful if you imagine an opponent while you perform. Imagining an opponent will help you throw your punches, strikes, and kicks at the proper heights. Learning katas is challenging, but performing them will help you combine motions and defend yourself against attacks from any direction.

Gekisai Dai Itchi kata

Although the motions in a kata are already set, a student must still use his or her own creativity to turn a kata into a graceful performance. This student is performing a motion from the Gekisai Dai Itchi kata.

Saifa

This student is performing
motions from the Saifa kata.

Sparring styles 空手

Sparring, or practice fighting, allows students to test their abilities against opponents. Sparring matches are always supervised by senseis. There are two main styles of sparring— **one-step sparring** and **free sparring**. In one-step sparring, two students perform an exercise using techniques that have been laid out by their sensei. To learn about free sparring, turn to pages 26 to 27. Sparring is an important part of each student's training. Fighting against opponents teaches students sportsmanship, fair play, and respect for other students. Sparring also helps students gain confidence in their abilities. It allows students to test their skills in a safe environment, under the watchful eye of a sensei.

No-contact sparring allows beginners to try sparring without the risk of injuring themselves or others.

No touching!

Beginner students perform **no-contact**, one-step sparring. During no-contact sparring, students must stop their motions before touching their opponents. These exercises are performed slowly and carefully. No-contact sparring teaches students to perform powerful, controlled motions. Eventually, students may begin to perform **light-contact** sparring. During light-contact sparring, they lightly strike their opponents. Turn to page 26 to learn about the equipment needed to perform light-contact sparring.

Step by step

To perform a one-step sparring exercise, you and your opponent stand facing each other. Before the match begins, bow to your opponent as a sign of respect. For each exercise, one student assumes the role of the attacker, and the other student acts in self-defense. The attacker steps toward the defender and performs a motion, which has been chosen by the sensei. The defender blocks the attack and performs a counterattack, which was also chosen by the sensei. Both you and your opponent must perform your motions correctly and with enough control so that you do not strike each other. After performing the exercise a few times, you and your opponent can switch roles.

Free sparring 空手

Free sparring is fast-paced sparring in which students do not use set exercises as they spar. During free-sparring matches, students must think on their feet, as they have no way of knowing which motions their opponents will perform. Free sparring is done only by advanced students. It requires students to bring together all they have learned about timing, control, and footwork. These skills help students anticipate the next motions their opponents will make. Free sparring also teaches students to respond quickly with appropriate motions.

Full-contact sparring

Some karate dojos allow students to practice **full-contact** free sparring. During full-contact free-sparring matches, students strike their opponents with full force. Usually, only students who are interested in taking part in competitions practice full-contact free sparring. Other students practice light-contact free sparring. Students should ask their sensei before trying full-contact free sparring.

To keep sparring matches safe, students must wear protective gear, which may include helmets, mouth guards, and pads to protect their hands and feet.

Free-sparring rules

Free sparring is challenging and can be dangerous for students, even when they are wearing protective gear. To reduce the risk of injuries, students must follow many rules while free sparring. During matches, they are not allowed to attack certain parts of their opponents' bodies, including their necks and eyes. Students are not permitted to make open-handed attacks on the faces of their opponents. Also, they are never allowed to grab or push their opponents in anger.

Weapons 空手

As the people of Okinawa developed their karate techniques, they sometimes used their farming and fishing tools as weapons. The Okinawan art of weaponry is known as *kobudo*. Although karate is empty-handed fighting, many of today's karate students are also trained to use weapons. The three main weapons with which karate students train are the *bo*, the *sai*, and the *tonfa*. Students are often taught to use weapons as they perform karate techniques they already know. For example, a student who knows how to perform an upper block can then be taught to perform an upper block using a tonfa. These pages show some common motions performed using karate weapons.

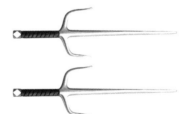

You can use your bo to perform a strike from back stance.

The sai is a weapon that was developed from a fishing tool used by Okinawan fishers.

The tonfa is a weapon that was developed from a tool used by Okinawan farmers to grind rice.

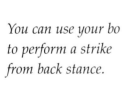

The bo is a weapon that was developed from a simple walking stick used by the Okinawan people.

*In horse stance, you can perform a **double block** using your sais. Proper concentration is essential.*

Tonfas are often used for blocking. This student is performing an upper block and a low block at the same time.

Karate competitions 空手

Some karate students may decide to test their sparring abilities at competitions. At competitions, students free spar against one another in pairs. Karate competitions test a student's skills, as well as his or her ability to maintain self-control in stressful situations.

During a match, a student earns points for every punch, strike, and kick that makes contact with a legal area of his or her opponent's body. Each technique must also be powerful and controlled. The student who earns the most points by the end of the match is the winner.

*During a karate competition, you must attack your opponent **aggressively**. Attacking aggressively means to attack over and over again with force.*

Kata competitions

Many students also take part in kata competitions. Kata competitions differ from sparring competitions in that they do not involve opponents. There are two kinds of kata competitions: empty-handed kata and weapons kata. Each student competes individually and must perform his or her motions in exactly the same way every time.

Good marks

A student is marked on how well his or her kata is performed. The student must be in total control of his or her motions. The motions must be performed with the correct technique and should show a great amount of energy, concentration, and enthusiasm. Judges of the competitions also look for coordination, proper breathing, balance, and good focus.

Students taking part in kata competitions must remain focused in order to perform all the motions in their katas correctly and energetically.

Glossary

Note: Boldfaced words that are defined in the text may not appear in the glossary.

combinations Two or more techniques performed one right after the other

counterattack A return attack performed by an athlete immediately after he or she has been attacked

deflect To force an opponent's technique to change direction

flex To contract a muscle, causing a joint to bend

free sparring Fast-paced sparring in which students do not use prearranged motions as they spar

match A contest between two students

opponent The person against whom a karate athlete competes during competitions and sparring matches

reaction The act of pulling back your opposite arm as your attacking arm is thrust forward

self-discipline The ability to control one's own actions

sport karate Karate that emphasizes preparation for competitions

stability The ability to hold a position

traditional karate Karate that emphasizes traditional self-defense

Index

1 2 3 4 5 6 7 8 9 0 Printed in the U.S.A. 4 3 2 1 0 9 8 7 6 5